Fact Finders®

ENDANGERED RAINFORESTS

INVESTIGATING RAINFORESTS IN CRISIS

Rani Iyer

raintree
a Capstone company — publishers for children

Raintree is an imprint of Capstone Global Library Limited, a company incorporated in England and Wales having its registered office at 264 Banbury Road, Oxford, OX2 7DY – Registered company number: 6695582

www.raintree.co.uk
myorders@raintree.co.uk

Editor: Abby Colich
Designer: Bobbie Nuytten
Media researcher: Gina Kammer
Original illustrations © Capstone Global Library Limited 2020
Production Specialist: Tori Abraham
Originated by Capstone Global Library Ltd
Printed and bound in India

ISBN 978 1 4747 9242 4 (hardback)
ISBN 978 1 4747 9250 9 (paperback)

British Library Cataloguing in Publication Data
A full catalogue record for this book is available from the British Library.

Acknowledgements
We would like to thank for the following for permission to use photographs: Corbis: Ashley Cooper, 22, Frans Lanting, 27, Karen Kasmauski, 15, Robert Harding World Imagery/Last Refuge, 7, Science Faction/Michele Westmorland, 8; Dreamstime: Pavol Kmeto, 6; Getty Images: Dorling Kindersley, 13, National Geographic/Randy Olson, 9; Nature Picture Library: Luiz Claudio Marigo, 25; Newscom: Minden Pictures/Michael & Patricia Fogden, 26, REUTERS/PAULO WHITAKER, 24; Science Source: NASA/Jessica Wilson, 23; Shutterstock: Andrew G. Davis, 21, Arina P Habich, 28, Banana Republic images, (background) cover, 1, Blend Images, 29, claffra, 20, Frontpage, 16, 18, gnomeandi, (bottom left) cover, guentermanaus, 5, Jan Mastnik, (top left) cover, Kirill Livshitskiy, (top right) cover, Lisette van der Hoorn, 19, nofilm2011, 4, Rich Carey, (bottom right) cover, Shi Yali, (top), 10, Stephane Bidouze, 12, sursad, 11, think4photop, 14, tristan tan, 17, wandee007, (bottom) 10.

We would like to thank our content consultant, Professor Gregory Gilbert of the Department of Environmental Studies at the University of California, Santa Cruz, USA, for his invaluable help in the preparation of this book.

Contents

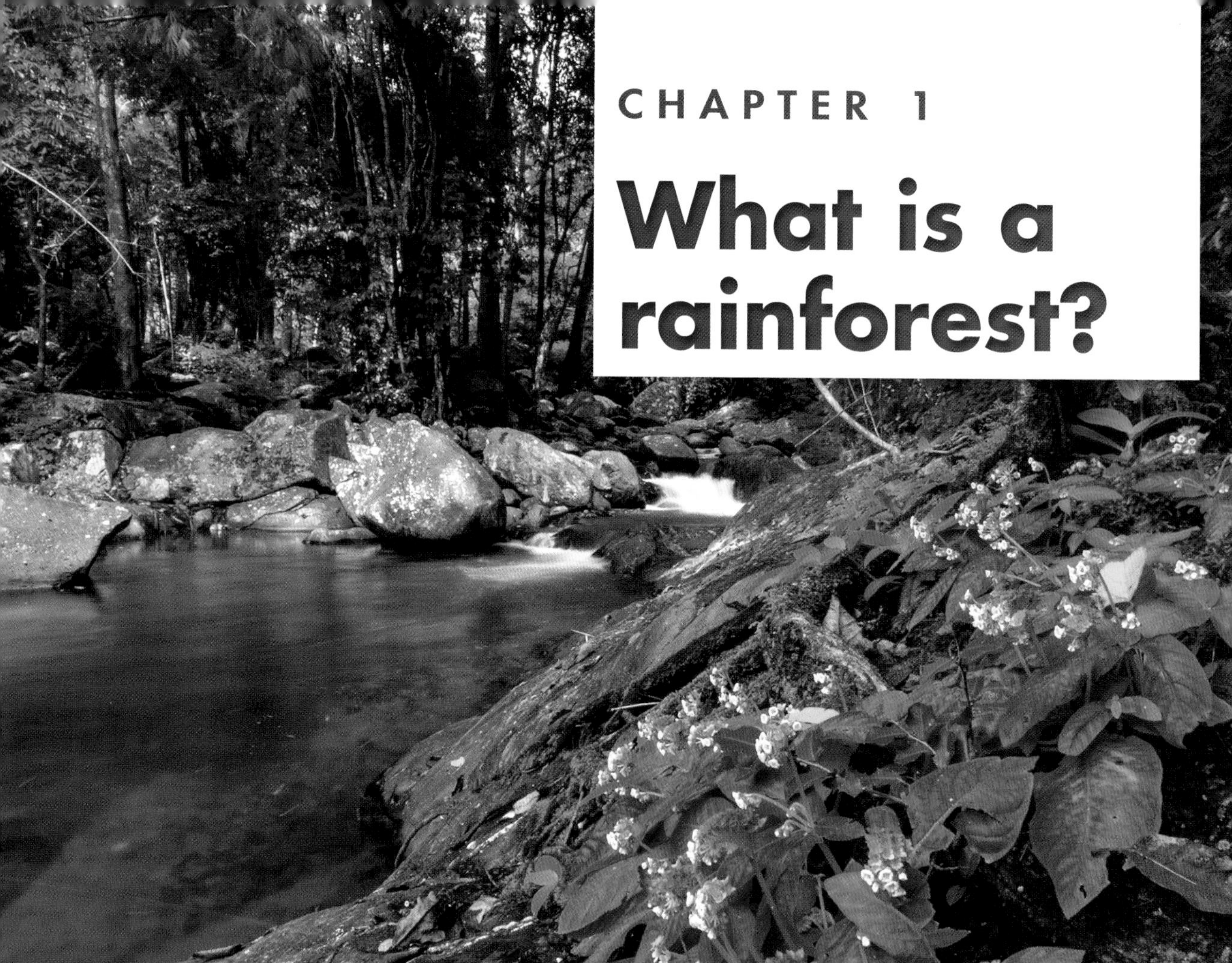

A stream flows through a rainforest in Thailand.

CHAPTER 1

What is a rainforest?

Enter into the warm and colourful tropical rainforest. Different shades of green are everywhere. Sounds of howling monkeys and croaking frogs come from all directions. Cool rain begins to fall.

Rainforests are rich with life. They are home to a huge number of **organisms**. Flowers and vines grow among the trees. Birds fly above. Snakes slide around below. Insects occupy the forest floor. Every living thing has its own role in this **ecosystem**.

organism living thing

ecosystem group of animals and plants that work together with their surroundings

Rainforests are not just beautiful and full of life. They are necessary for the planet. Life on Earth depends on the rainforest in many ways.

Today rainforests all over the world are in danger of disappearing. People are cutting and burning down rainforest trees at a rapid rate. These actions destroy plant and animal habitats and have an impact on the whole planet. But people can stop the destruction if they are careful. Protecting and saving the rainforests takes a global effort.

A damaged part of a rainforest in Brazil

What's in a rainforest?

Most rainforests are tropical rainforests. These forests grow near the **equator**. They are wet and warm all year round. They grow in Central and South America, Africa, Asia and Australia.

Rainforest trees grow to different heights. Canopy trees are big and tall, shading the other trees. Emergent trees shoot out above the canopy. Sub-canopy trees grow just under the canopy. Below the sub-canopy are the understorey trees. More plants grow along the forest floor.

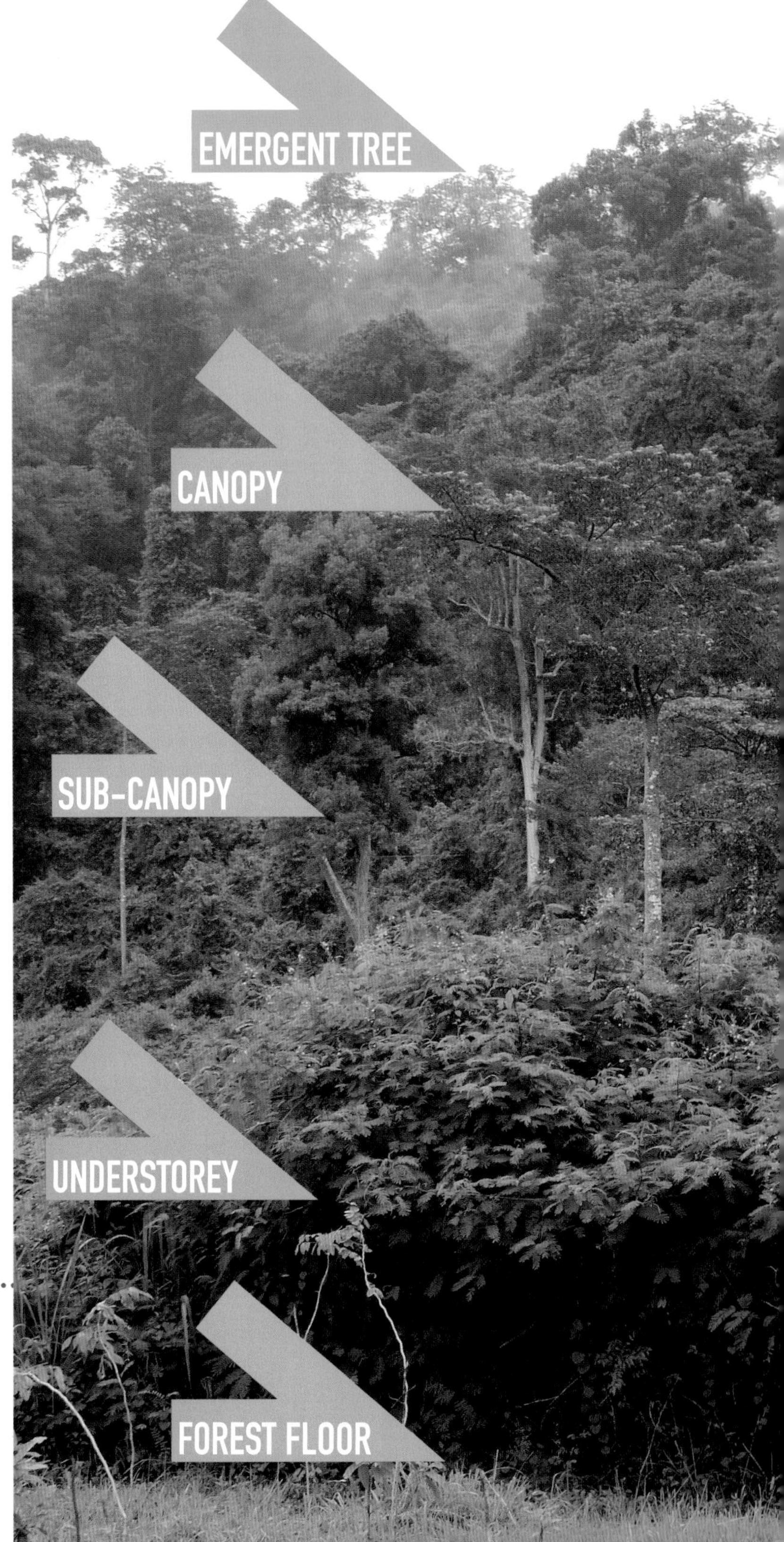

Each layer of the rainforest supports different life forms.

Rainforest life

Only 2 per cent of Earth is covered by rainforests, but they house at least 50 per cent of all known plants and animals. Some **species** live in only one area and are found nowhere else on Earth. The termite-trapping pitcher plant grows in only one location in Malaysia. Mountain gorillas live only near the forest bordering Congo and Uganda. If one of these species dies out in one forest, it is lost forever.

FACT

Scientists believe the Earth is home to about 8.7 million species. Only 1.2 million species have been discovered. It could take up to 1,200 years to record the rest of Earth's species.

equator imaginary line around the middle of the Earth
species group of living things with similar features

A group of gorillas in the rainforest in Rwanda

CHAPTER 2
Rainforests are important

A young woman working in the rainforest in Papua New Guinea

Rainforests are important to people around the world, even to those who don't live near one. They provide many necessities, including food, clean air and water.

Living in the rainforest

Nearly 50 million people live in tropical rainforests. The Huli of Papua New Guinea, the Yanomami of South America and Mbuti of Africa rely on the rainforest for survival. Their food, clothing and shelter come from the rainforest. When human actions destroy or harm the rainforest, it threatens these people and their way of life.

The Mbuti people

For the Mbuti people of Africa, the rainforest is their home. Adult Mbuti are rarely taller than 150 centimetres (5 feet). Their height makes them well adapted to live deep in the rainforest. They live in small **nomadic** groups. For shelter they weave leaves and saplings into huts. They often use leaves for clothing. Families visit nearby villages to trade **bushmeat** and other rainforest products. In exchange they get tapioca, salt and other produce. The loss of rainforests is threatening the Mbuti way of life. As forests are cut down for mining and logging, the Mbuti are driven away from their homes.

nomadic travelling from place to place without a permanent home

bushmeat meat from wild animals used for food

Mbuti women

Rainforest for everyone

Many foods originate from rainforests. These include nuts such as cashews, and vegetables such as peppers. Palm oil is used for cooking and other products (see page 17). Fruits such as pineapples, mangoes and avocados were once wild rainforest plants. If rainforests are not protected, the world could lose the wild relatives of these plants.

Red mango fruit

Twenty-five per cent of the world's medicine comes from rainforest plants. Quinine, which comes from the bark of the cinchona tree, helps to cure malaria. Other plant extracts are used in anti-cancer drugs.

A man harvests palm fruit used for its oil.

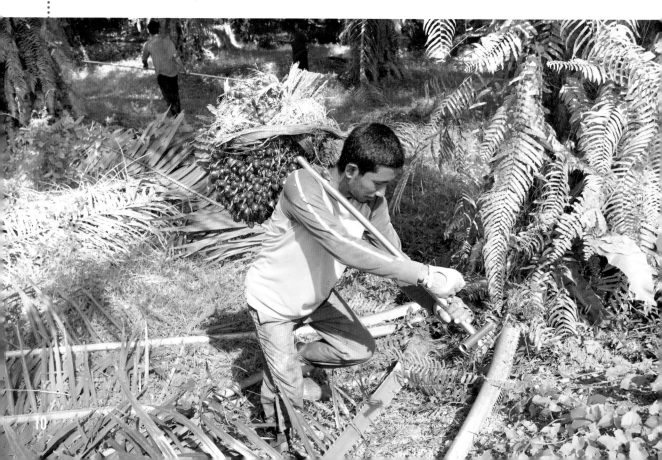

Chocolate at risk

Chocolate is made from the seeds of cacao trees. These trees are native to parts of the Amazon rainforest. For centuries, ancient peoples made a drink with cocoa beans. Beginning in the 16th century, cocoa farming spread around the world. Today cacao trees are grown on farms, mostly in Africa. However, the farmed trees often die from diseases and pests. Scientists are studying the wild relatives of cocoa in rainforests of the Amazon. The wild plants may offer clues that could help protect all cacao trees.

Cacao tree

Cool planet

Rainforests help keep the Earth's temperature in balance. Most living things take in the gas oxygen. They produce the gas carbon dioxide. Carbon dioxide is also released into the air when humans use certain fuels. This extra carbon dioxide can warm the Earth too much. It increases the planet's **greenhouse effect**. Even a slight rise in temperature can cause changes in **climate** that put life on Earth in danger. During **photosynthesis** plants take in carbon dioxide. They then release oxygen back into the air. Large rainforest trees are best at taking in carbon dioxide. This helps to prevent **climate change** caused by too much carbon dioxide in the air.

Fog covers this rainforest in Thailand.

Rainforest rain

Rainforests help to provide rain for the whole planet. Rainforests have more plants than other areas on Earth. All these plants absorb warmth from the Sun. When plants warm up, they release moisture into the air. Eventually this moisture forms clouds and rain falls. The rainfall refills rivers that provide water for plants, animals and people. Many of the world's largest rivers flow through the rainforests. The Amazon **basin** alone contains 20 per cent of all the freshwater in the world.

greenhouse effect warming effect that happens when certain gases in the Earth's atmosphere absorb heat and make the air warmer

climate average weather patterns of a certain place throughout the year

photosynthesis process by which green plants make food using sunlight and carbon dioxide

climate change significant change in Earth's climate over a period of time

basin area of land around a river from which water drains into the river

Rainforest water cycle

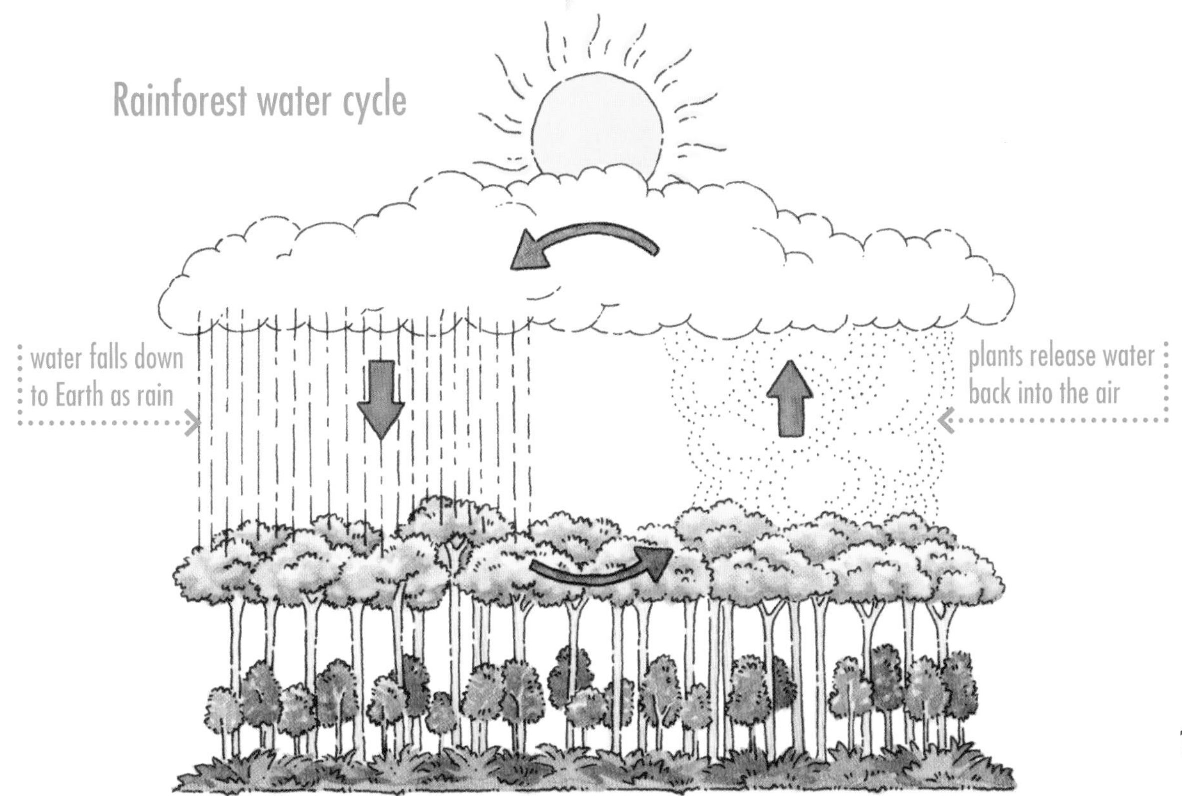
water falls down to Earth as rain
plants release water back into the air

CHAPTER 3

It was once a rainforest

Bare land is left in an area where rainforest once stood in Thailand.

Humans are destroying rainforests at an alarming rate. Experts say that about 32,000 hectares (80,000 acres) of rainforest are lost each day. All over the world, rainforests are cleared to make room for farming, mining and building dams. Roads, homes and cities stand where rainforests once did.

Deforestation

Deforestation is the large destruction of a forest by cutting or burning down trees. When a forest is clear-cut, all the trees in one area are cut down. Other plants are also destroyed. Surviving animals must find new places to live. The cleared area is often used for farming. After a few years, the soil can no longer support the crops. Farmers must find new land. Sometimes forest can regrow in these areas, but the process is slow.

Slash and burn

Sometimes farmers clear land by cutting down rainforest trees and plants and then burning the area. Sometimes this "slash and burn" process is used for small areas. Ashes from the fire provide nutrients for the crops for three to five years. Then the land is left behind. Some forest plants may be able to regrow.

Other times slash and burn happens too frequently or covers too large an area. The fires release harmful extra carbon dioxide into the air. There are then fewer trees left to absorb this gas. The smoke also adds to air and water **pollution**. After the land is left behind, the soil **erodes**, making it difficult for plant life to regrow.

pollution harmful materials that damage the air, water and soil

erode to wear away

Haze covers an area of destroyed rainforest in Guatemala.

Farms and plantations

Large companies buy parts of rainforest land all over the world. The land is cleared to plant crops such as palms, coffee, tea and soya beans. In addition to the loss of rainforest, these crops need a lot of water. Water supplies run low. The crops also absorb less carbon dioxide than rainforest trees. Extra carbon dioxide builds up in the air.

Rainforests are also cleared to plant trees that are used to make paper. After the trees are cut down to make paper, the land is replanted again and again with the same tree species. This changes the soil and makes it more difficult for native species to regrow later.

A large soya bean field next to the rainforest in Brazil

Orangutan loss

Palm oil is used in food, such as biscuits, and to make cosmetics, such as shampoo and soap. In recent years the demand for palm oil has risen. To keep up with the demand, farmers in Southeast Asia clear rainforest land to plant more palms. Orangutans depend on the rainforest in this area for survival. With nowhere to go, the orangutan population in this area has been cut in half.

An oil palm plantation

Ranches

Animals are raised for human food on ranches. In Brazil, millions of cattle are raised on land that was once the Amazon rainforest. In addition to the loss of rainforest, cattle produce gas that fills the air with greenhouse gases. With less forest, there are fewer trees producing oxygen and cleaning the air.

Cattle now graze a field that sits where a rainforest was recently slashed and burned.

A rainforest is logged on the island of Borneo.

Logging

Logging is another land use that destroys rainforest. Loggers cut down rainforest trees. The wood is used for furniture, flooring and building materials. It is also used for paper and paper products. Only certain tree species are cut down, but the whole forest is still affected. Losing one kind of tree makes it more difficult for species dependent on trees to survive. Fewer plants and animals can live in these areas.

Mining

Many rainforests grow in areas that are rich in metals, minerals or gemstones. Miners clear the rainforest and then blast the land open. Once destroyed, forest cannot regrow on this land. When an area is blasted, dust particles remain in the air. This dust affects the breathing of people and animals. Soil erodes causing landslides. **Run-off** pollutes nearby rivers.

run-off water that flows over land instead of soaking into the ground

Oil

Some rainforests grow on top of areas rich in oil. The oil is used to make petrol and other fuels. Miners drill deep into the Earth to reach the oil. Usually the rainforest is cleared before drilling can begin. The materials and process used to drill for oil can pollute the land, water and air. Some of the oil is spilt or illegally dumped. This can be harmful to life in the area.

FACT

In the 1970s and 1980s, an American company drilled for oil in part of the Ecuadoran rainforest. The company used cheap products during oil drilling. As a result, toxins polluted the soil and water. Local people believe this led them to develop many health problems, including cancer.

An oil rig in a rainforest

This dam is also used as a public swimming pool.

Development

When rainforests are destroyed for farming and mining, nearby areas must be developed. Roads are built through the rainforest to reach the farms and mines. New cities are built for people to live close to their place of work. **Dams** are built to collect and store water. These dams destroy land and water habitats.

dam barrier built across a river or stream to hold back water

CHAPTER 4
Global ripples

New planted trees begin to grow in an area that was deforested.

Loss of the rainforest causes a wide range or problems for the whole planet. It's more than a matter of losing trees and plants. Air and water are damaged. People, animals and all life are affected.

Loss of rainforest life

Rainforests are home to many species, including several that are **endangered**. When rainforests are destroyed, species lose part of their habitats. Species either do not survive the destruction or must move into a smaller area. Often a species cannot survive in a smaller area and the population **declines**. Scientists say it's possible for some species to die out before they are even discovered.

endangered at risk of dying out

FACT

How long does it take a rainforest to regrow? When land in a rainforest is used for farming, the soil is only good for a few years. After farmers leave, a rainforest can take up to about 50 years to regrow. If some trees are left in place while the land is used for farming, rainforests can grow back within 20 years.

Areas of tropical rainforest are coloured in bright green.

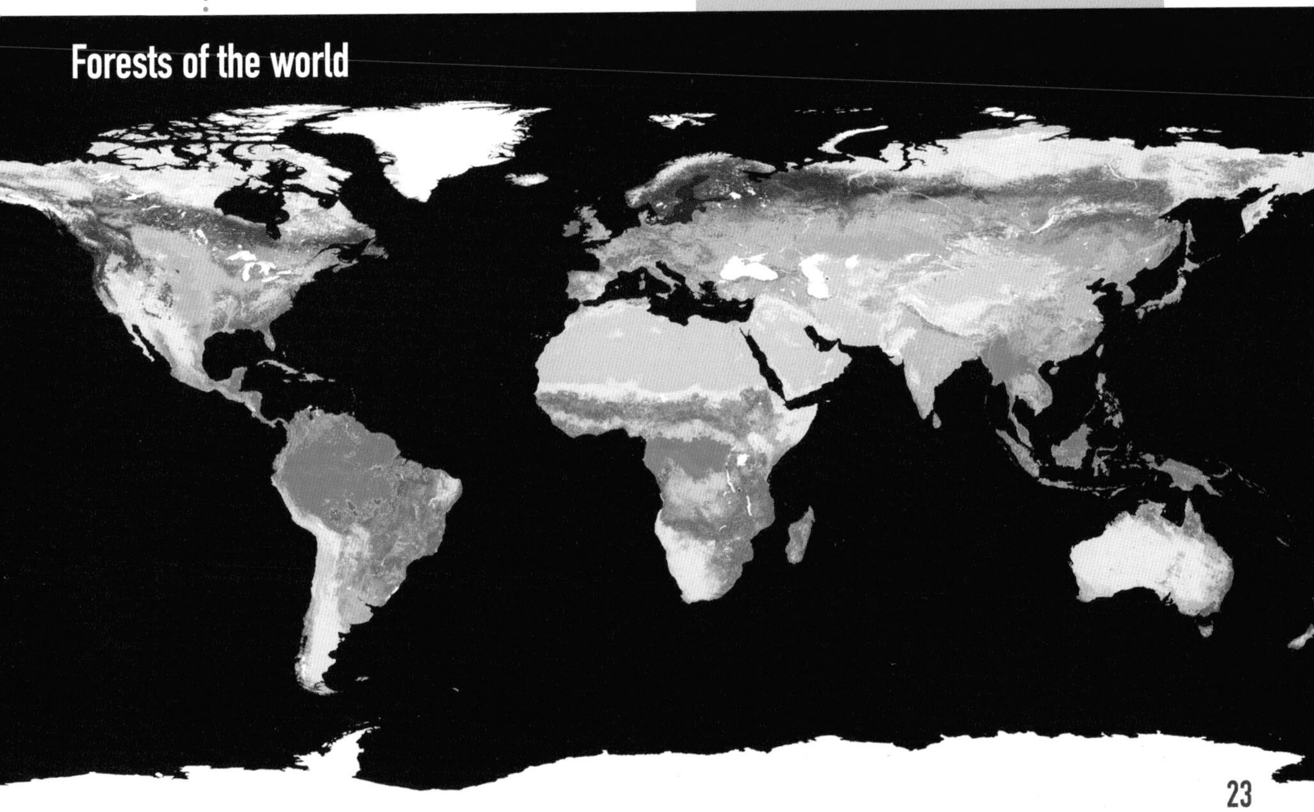

A warmer planet

Loss of rainforest also affects the world's climate. When old, large trees are cut down, they release carbon dioxide into the air. Every year tons of carbon is released into the air during deforestation. Carbon dioxide and other harmful gases are also released when people drive cars and use electricity. With the loss of so many trees, there are fewer of them to absorb this excess carbon dioxide.

Carbon dioxide and other harmful gases become trapped in the air. These gases cause Earth's temperature to rise. Warmer temperatures on Earth can cause polar ice to melt, areas to flood and entire ecosystems to be disrupted.

These dead fish are one result of drought caused by Amazon deforestation.

Less rainfall

Rainforest trees play an important role in the Earth's water cycle. They add water to the atmosphere. This helps to form clouds that make rain. The more rainforest trees are cut down, the less moisture is released into the air. Less water is available to make rain. Less rain can cause drought and even more rainforest life to die.

drought long period of weather with little or no rainfall

Less rainfall affects life outside the rainforest too. Moisture created by the rainforest travels around the globe. When Earth loses rainforest trees, there's less rainfall across the entire planet. This can lead to **droughts**.

This part of the Amazon River has dried up.

CHAPTER 5

Saving the rainforest

People around the world are working together to save the rainforests. Several organizations are dedicated to preserving this important ecosystem. What needs to happen to keep the rainforests from disappearing? People who study rainforests believe that governments, scientists and citizens need to work together.

Forest regrowth

With the right protection and support, smaller cleared areas can regrow. Scientists are working to help some areas grow back. It takes several years and there is often less life there than in the original forests. But the more plants that regrow, the cleaner air will be.

Ecotourism

Ecotourism programmes can help protect the rainforest and provide for people who live in them. These tours of delicate areas do not disturb the land. The money charged goes towards supporting and protecting the forest. Ecotourism also helps local residents by employing them as guides.

Tourists view the rainforest in Costa Rica

Loquillo research station

For 30 years scientists have carefully studied the rainforest at the Loquillo Long-Term Ecological Research station (LUQ) in Puerto Rico. The studies show that rainforests recover faster from natural changes than from the damage caused by humans. Scientists also study the ways rainforests impact human life.

Research and studies

Scientists maintain permanent plots in rainforests to study the many organisms. Several ongoing, long-term studies will give scientists clues about how rainforests adjust to climate changes.

A scientist measures a large Rafflesia flower in the rainforest on the island of Borneo.

Everyone can help

Most people do not live near a rainforest, but their choices always have an impact on the environment. Here are some things people can do that will help protect rainforests.

Use less paper and recycle the paper after it is used. Write on the other side of paper before throwing it away. Buy recycled paper.

Buy food, including meat, from local farmers. This will stop support for food produced on farms created by deforestation. Also avoid buying products that contain palm oil.

Avoid buying new furniture made of rosewood, ebony or mahogany. These woods are obtained from tropical rainforest.

Walk or cycle to nearby places instead of driving. This helps keep the air clean.

Research and learn more about rainforests. Find a trusted organization to donate money to or find another way to help.

Rainforests are in trouble. But there is still hope. When people work together and everyone plays their part, damage can be reversed. The remaining rainforests will be protected. The entire planet will benefit.

Cycling rather than driving is one way to help keep the Earth clean.

Glossary

basin area of land around a river from which water drains into the river

bushmeat meat from wild animals used for food

climate average weather patterns of a certain place throughout the year

climate change significant change in Earth's climate over a period of time

dam barrier built across a river or stream to hold back water

decline become smaller

drought long period of weather with little or no rainfall

ecosystem group of animals and plants that work together with their surroundings

endangered at risk of dying out

equator imaginary line around the middle of the Earth

erode to wear away

greenhouse effect warming effect that happens when certain gases in the Earth's atmosphere absorb heat and make the air warmer

nomadic travelling from place to place without a permanent home

organism living thing

photosynthesis process by which green plants make food using sunlight and carbon dioxide

pollution harmful materials that damage the air, water and soil

run-off water that flows over land instead of soaking into the ground

species group of living things with similar features

Comprehension questions

1. How is life changing for people who live in rainforests? What adaptations and changes to their lives must they make? How is this different from what people who live outside of rainforests are experiencing?

2. To best protect the rainforest, what problem affecting it do you think must be solved first? Use information from the text and other sources to support your answer.

3. Reread page 6 and study the photograph and labels. What types of rainforest life do you think are best suited for each layer?

Find out more

Natural Resources (Ecographics), Izzi Howell (Franklin Watts, 2019)

Rainforests (Explorer Travel Guides), Nick Hunter (Raintree, 2013)

Rainforests (The World's Biomes), Kimberly Sidabras (Raintree, 2018)

Rainforests (Where on Earth?), Susie Brooks (Wayland, 2016)

Rainforests in 30 Seconds, Dr Jen Green (Ivy Kids, 2017)

The Amazon (DK Eyewitness), DK (DK Publishing, 2015)

Websites

Visit this website for a simple explanation of the greenhouse effect:
climatekids.nasa.gov/greenhouse-effect/

Visit this CBBC website for information about greenhouse gases, global warming and the ozone layer, and what you can do to help the planet:
news.bbc.co.uk/cbbcnews/hi/find_out/guides/world/global_warming/newsid_1575000/1575441.stm

DKfindout! has information about rainforests on its website:
dkfindout.com/uk/animals-and-nature/habitats-and-ecosystems/amazon-rainforest/

Index